Ink &
Constellations

Ishita Arora

BookLeaf
Publishing

India | USA | UK

Presentation by *BookLeaf Publishing*

Web: www.bookleafpub.com

E-mail: info@bookleafpub.com

ISBN: 9789360948191

First edition 2024

This collection is dedicated to the intrepid souls who dare to dream, the steadfast hearts who dance beneath the celestial canopy, and the discerning minds who seek solace within the eloquent script of existence. With profound gratitude and admiration, I extend this offering to those who champion the pursuit of truth, uphold the sanctity of individuality, and embody the essence of empathy. May these verses serve as luminous beacons amidst life's darkest hours, and may the celestial constellations woven into these pages illuminate the path of self-discovery for all who journey within.

ACKNOWLEDGEMENT

I extend my deepest gratitude to all those who have contributed to the creation of "Ink & Constellations." Firstly, I want to express my heartfelt appreciation to my family and friends for their unwavering support and encouragement throughout this journey. Your belief in my creative endeavors has been a constant source of inspiration.

I am profoundly grateful to my readers, whose enthusiasm and appreciation fuel my passion for writing. Your engagement with my work is truly humbling, and I am honored to share these poems with you.

A special thank you to my editor and publishing team for their dedication and expertise in bringing this collection to fruition. Your guidance and professionalism have been invaluable.

I am also indebted to the poets and artists who have influenced and inspired me over the years. Your work has shaped my artistic vision and enriched the pages of "Ink & Constellations."

Last but not least, I would like to express my deepest appreciation to the muse that resides within me, guiding my pen and igniting my creativity. Without your presence, these poems would remain but whispers in the wind.

Thank you, from the bottom of my heart, for being a part of this journey.

With sincere appreciation,
Ishita Arora

PREFACE

Welcome to "Ink & Constellations," a collection of poetry that invites you on a journey through the depths of human emotion and the boundless expanse of the universe. Within these pages lie 71 verses that delve into the intricacies of friendship, the intoxicating essence of love, and the relentless pursuit of dreams and ambitions.

As you embark on this poetic odyssey, you'll encounter themes that resonate with the struggles and triumphs of the human experience. From the burdens imposed by society to the hypocrisy that taints our world, each poem serves as a mirror reflecting the complexities of our existence.

Yet, amidst the chaos and turmoil, there is beauty to be found. Through the lens of poetic expression, we discover moments of profound insight and inspiration, reminding us of the resilience within us all. These poems are not merely words on a page; they are beacons of hope guiding us through life's darkest moments.

I invite you to immerse yourself in these verses' rich tapestry of emotions. May "Ink & Constellations" ignite your imagination, stir your

soul, and leave an indelible mark upon your
heart.

Warm regards,
Ishita Arora

TABLE OF CONTENTS

Life's Tapestry

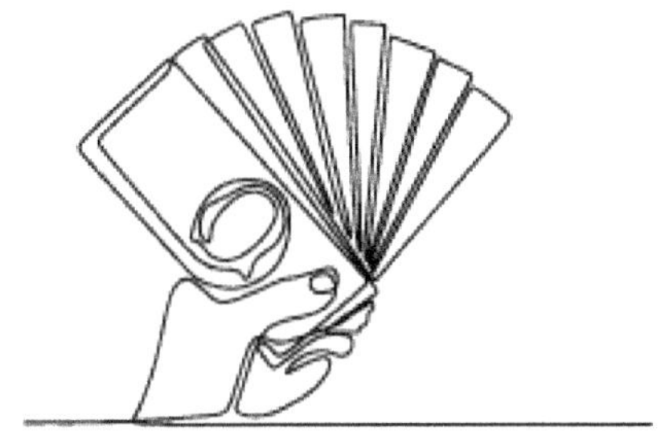

Dreamweaver's Tapestry: A Symphony of Lucid Dreams

In realms of twilight, when sleep softly weaves,
Where dreams and reality gently converge,
There lies a realm where the mind believes,
In lucid depths, where imaginations surge.

Through veils of slumber, consciousness takes flight,
In dreams unfettered by earthly bounds,
Where the soul wanders in the dead of night,
And the mind's eye paints worlds without bounds.

In lucid dreams, the ordinary fades,
As stars cascade in rivers of light,
Where the impossible dances and parades,
And the mundane surrenders to the night.

Oh, what wonders await in this mystic land,
Where thoughts are the architects of delight,
And the dreamer holds the reins in hand,
Guiding destiny through the velvet night.

Yet, tread with care, for in this realm of dreams,
The line 'twixt reality and fantasy thins,
For though the spirit soars on silent streams,
The waking world beckons, where true life
begins.

So cherish the gift of lucid dreaming's art,
A canvas where the soul's colors gleam,
In the silent chambers of the dreaming heart,
Where reality and fantasy dance in a dream.

Whispers of an Empathic Heart

In a world of noise, you feel the breeze,
A heart that beats with empathy's ease.
Sensitive soul, you see beyond the veil,
Where others skim, your depth prevails.

You feel the whispers of the wind's soft call,
Emotions dance like leaves in fall.
Love blooms fierce within your chest,
Each feeling, a treasure, you hold it blessed.

Misunderstood by those who can't perceive,
Your empathy, a gift, they cannot conceive.
Intuitive to every vibe, every hue,
You navigate life with a soul so true.

In your sensitivity, strength does reside,
A wellspring of emotions, deep and wide.
So cherish this gift, though it brings pain,
For it's what makes you beautifully humane.

Embracing Demons: Through Light and Dark

In Angel's and in Devil's flight,
Within us, dwell both dark and light.
God's presence, I'm not quite sure,
But demons lurk, that much is pure.

Some lie deep, within our souls,
While others steer, our life's whole.
These demons, not all are bad,
They push us forth, when times are sad.

Without their nudge, we might not strive,
For success, for dreams, to thrive.
But heed their power, know their range,
For unchecked, they could bring change.

In this world, where selfishness reigns,
And greed's the fuel for many gains,
Others pull you down, with glee,
When you falter, they feel free.

They'll flaunt their feats, and criticize,
When you fall short, it's no surprise.
Yet within us, demons dwell,
To fend off those who wish us hell.

They spur us on, to claim our place,
In every realm, every race.
For those who sow these seeds of doubt,
Are the same who feed our inner shout.

So let us wield our demons wise,
With limits set, to reach the skies.
For in this world, both dark and bright,
We navigate, with inner light.

Gaslighter's Groan

How dare you spill my secrets, oh so bold,
And tarnish the image that I carefully mold?
You've exposed my truth, how could you be so
mean?
Just trying to keep my slate squeaky clean.

I manipulate and twist, with words I'm sly,
Yet you dare to call me out? Oh my, oh my!
I'm the victim here, can't you see?
Stop making a fuss, just let me be free!

I'll play the victim, shed a tear or two,
But it's you who's at fault, not me, it's true!
You ruined my reputation with your truth-telling
game,
That's how it goes when you play with my fame.

So, next time, think twice before you reveal,
The deeds and the words that I try to conceal.
I'll continue to charm and deceive with my lies,
But remember, it's you who's the jerk in their
eyes!

Pehchan ka Sawal

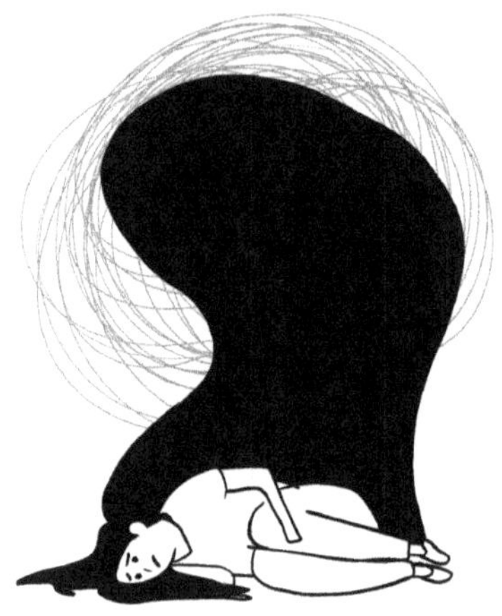

Kyun?

Socha hai kabhi?
Kya koi sochta hai kabhi?
Waqt beet ta chala jaata hai,
Baatein shor banne lagti hain,
Chehre aankhon mein chubhne lagte hain,
Betiyan bojh lagne lagti hain.

Aisa lagta hai jaise, sab kuch
Sab kuch jhoot ki bunyaad par bana tha,
Ab tak. Jaise bas waqt beet raha tha,
Aur waqt bitane ke liye jo zaroori tha,
Wahi kar rahe the sab.

Aisa lagta hai, jo hamesha bolte the
Bolte the ki bahut pyaar hai.
Aisa lagta hai ab, jhoot bolte the sab.

Kyun? Kyun koi bas palla jhaadna chahta hai?
Ladki hoon na.
Peechha chhudana chahte hain sab,
Itna mushkil hota hai kya ladki hona?
Itni mushkilein hoti hain kya?

Na chup rahne se?
Main poochhti hoon akhir kyun chup rahna hai?
Main poochhti hoon...
Kyun sab kuch chup chaap sahna hai?
Kyun sab kuch chup chaap jhelna hai?
Kyun bas baat ko maanna hai?
Kyun? Kyun ladki hona hai?
Kyun beti hona hai?

Aaj tak nahi lagta tha kabhi.
Kabhi nahi laga ki beti hona itna bojh ho sakta
hai.
Ab kabhi kabhi lagta hai...
Ki ya to beta hoti,
Ya paida hote hi mar jaati,
Ab bade hokar ye sunna
"Mar ja"—ye kaunsa achha hai?

Bhaag jaao lagta hai kabhi kabhi,
Khush rahoongi bahut akeli, ye bhi jaanti hoon,
Par sukoon se kahan rahne denge apne hi log,
Khatkega inko woh sab kuch.
Sab kuch jo apne liye achha karti hoon,
Soch chhoti hain inki, samjhein ge nahi.
Jeena chahti hoon main khul ke,
Mujhe to jeena hai,
Par in bandishon mein nahi.

Sangharsh ki Dhun

Kya jeetna itna zaroori hai?
Roz chalte hain, daudte hain,
Is samaj ki gehrayion mein,
Kahin hum khud se bhi kho jate hain.

Insan ne shayad kudrat se kuch nahi seekha,
Kudrat ne insan ko banaya zaroor hai,
Par ye samaj... ye toh insan ki den hai,
Jahan har kadam pe naye raaste hai.

Jeetna, haar ke sath chalna,
Daur samajh ke, insaniyat ka safar,
Har karz chukana, har rukawat ko paar karna,
Zindagi ki iss jung mein, har lamha hai ek
imtehaan.

Kya jeetna itna zaroori hai?
Shayad hai, lekin haar bhi ek faasla hai,

Kyun na chalain hum safar mein,
Ek doosre ki madad se, ek doosre ka saath
nibhate hue.

Zid ki Khoj

Zindagi ka safar, har chal aur parvat,
Khwaabon ki bulandiyon par, har mushkil ka
saamna kiya.
Apnon ka saath na mila, par zid ne rasta
dikhaya,
Zindagi ka maksad hai, apni zid ko pura karna hi
pyaara.

Zid ke bina, zindagi thi adhoori,
Zindagi ka arth hai, sangharsh aur zid ki jhanki
bhari.
Zid ne hi dikhaya safalta ka manzar,
Agar zid na hoti, zindagi hoti bebas ek safar.

Apne aap ko bachana, zindagi ko jeena hai,
Koshish kar rahe hain hum, apne sapno ko paane mein.
Khoob ladaiyan ladhi hain, sikhi hain humne kuch nayi baatein,
Ab uth chuki hoon, nayi raahon pe chalne ka hai iraada humein.

Bandishein

Chalo chalein kahin...
Jahan koi bandishein nahin,
Chalo chalein kahin
Jahan bas khwahishein ho pali.

Chalo chalein kahin...
Jahan ho khula asman,
Chalo chalein kahin
Jahan tum khud banao, sajao apna jahan.

Chalo chalein kahin...
Jahan samajh ke jhoote dayre na ho,
Chalo chalein kahin
Jahan sach ke nam par jhoot bikta na ho.

Chalo chalein kahin...
Jahan khokhle na ho alfaaz,
Chalo chalein kahin
Jahan na ho koi raaz.

Chalo chalein wahin...
Jahan bas khushiyan ho bhari,
Chalo chalein wahin
Jahan koi bandishein nahin.

Death Comes Alive

One day I was thinking along with my coffee
Why is death always ready to be…? A setting
sun, a no-moon night
A dying flower… or closed twinkling eyes.
Whenever it comes… it brings along with it
sorrow and agony
But in some places…
There are some reasons for her to make merry.
Death always comes giving a sign
But it never asks us to give others a bit of time.
We keep on denying death… and believe in
remaining alive

Death defeats life in the battle… and comes to
us making others cry.
I wonder why people are afraid of death!
Why do they fear to die?
Though it's a matter of fact,
A thing that is born will someday get destroyed.
Reason being any, it will silently come
And ask for our company,
Till heaven or hell
Till the time, Death rings the last bell.
We go on and on… and our life gets over,
We go across… and death comes closer
We are received by death…
And seen off by life
The only matter of life being… that
Death Comes Alive.

Flowers and Footsteps

Amidst life's strange symphony,
Time's pendulum swings with grace,
Yet in our frantic hustle,
We lose sight of each other's face.
Moments pass with quiet fury,
Connections made, then abruptly fleeting,
Like flowers trampled underfoot,
In the swift dance of greeting and parting.

This enigma, unfathomable,
Defies the bounds of prophetic sight.
I ponder, amidst the cacophony,
How do some hold onto the Light?

Two tribes amidst life's tapestry,
One masks pain in stoic veneer,
While the other, in seeking validation,
Magnifies every painful tear.

In this dichotomy's realm,
Let's turn to heads, the child's innocence,
Where simplicity reigns and truth makes sense.
In their laughter, in their play,
Lies wisdom lost in grown-up fray.

For in the heart of innocence lies,
A beacon true, untouched by lies.
They see the world with untainted eyes,
Where love and joy forever rise.

So amidst life's confusion, its endless chase,
Let's embrace the childlike grace.
For in their light, we find our way,
Guided by hope, come what may.

HAAR GAYE TOH KYA?

Akele mein shayad roz sochti hu…
akhir ye jeet kya hai?
roz hi dikhti h is zindagi ki asmanjas…
kya sach mein… is zindagi mein kuch naya hai?

Waqt beetta chala jata hai,
aage toh roz badhte hai hum…
Par is jeet ki talash mein
roz kahin kho se jate hai hum?

Har jagah, har peher, har pal mein
Jeet ke liye kyu karni hai ladai?
aisa nahi hai ki ladna bura hai
Nahi! Par ladte ladte
Khud ko kho dena konsa bhala hai?

Khud ko bhoolkar…
Har din aage badhkar
Mehnat toh karte hai hum
par roz sirhane jakar…
Wo 'kuch' jo khota hai roz humse
Use dhundne ki koshish kyu karte hai hum?

Har koi jeet hasil karne ko kehta hai,
Har koi sabse aage rehne ko kehta hai
sab jeetne ki naseehat toh dete hain…
par koi ye kyu nahi batata kabhi
Ki haar gaye toh kya hai?

Kabhi kabhi lagta hai
ki ek kafas mein band hain hum…
Agar jeet hasil hui
toh rihayee mil jayegi,
Warna isi kafas mein kaid rahenge hum.

Bat to tab chubhti hai dil par…
Jab ehsas hota hai, ki har koi hasil karna chahta
hai jeet,
par sochne ki baat ye hai janab
Jeet har kisi ko milti kahan hai?

Milegi bhi bhala kaise…
Yaha jeet ke liye daud kam kahan hai?
Khair mudda zindagi ki haar jeet ka bhi nahi,
Mudda to dil harne ka hai.
Khud ko nakam samajhke
Daud chodne ka hai!

Naseehat nahi sach sunati hu aj…
Harne ya jeetne wale se
Koshish karne wala bada hai!

Jeet gaye toh banane wale ka shukr kar…
Haar gaye toh bnane wale par aitmaad kar.
Ye haar jeet ka silsila toh na khatm hua hai kbhi
na kbhi hoga
Janna toh tujhe hai, manna bhi tujhe hai,
Is haar jeet se zindagi bahut hai upar!

Toh ab ye sochna zarur…
ki ye jeet nahi toh kya?
Sochna zarur…
ki har gaye toh kyaa
Gaur karna zarur…
ki kho gaye toh kya?
Sochna zarur….
ki haar gaye toh kya?

Embracing Blessings

In the shadow of trauma, it's tough to let go,
Rewiring your brain, it moves oh so slow.
But blessings are real, and good folks are near,
A softer life waits, don't let fear steer.

Nobody tells of this hard inner fight,
To trust once more, to let in the light.
But blessings are out there, just waiting for you,
Good people and kindness, they're not few.

So take a deep breath, let the healing begin,
Open your heart, let the love flow in.
A softer life, with its gentle embrace,
Let it happen, find your peace, find your place.

Authentic Revelations

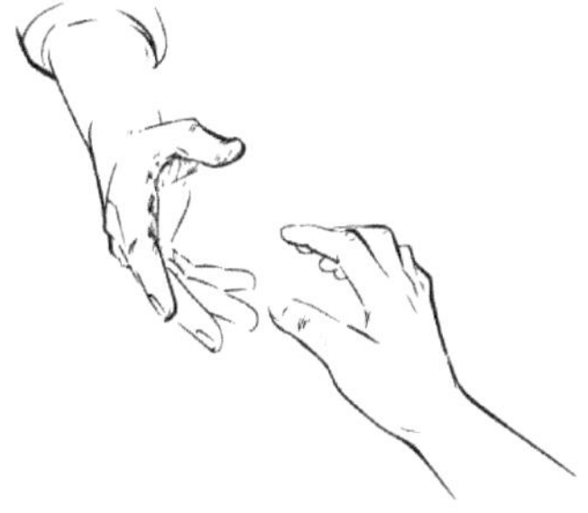

In this world, a tapestry of souls unfurls,
Some speak not, lost in silent swirls.
Why shy away, avoiding truth's clear shout?
Hesitation's grip, casting shadows of doubt.

Directness fades, obscured by fear's veil,
Yet clarity's absence leaves hearts frail.
For in the echo of unspoken words,
Relationships falter, like fragile birds.

Material gleam blinds some in its sway,
Travel, jewels, and displays hold sway.
But beneath the glimmer, what do we find?
A hollow echo in the heart's confines.

Manipulation's art, a twisted game,
Disguised as prowess, hiding shame.
Competitive spirits, blind to others' rise,
Their joy is eclipsed by envy's guise.

Yet amidst the chaos, a beacon bright,
Those earthy souls, in fearless light.
Despite the world's attempts to quell,
Their power shines an unyielding spell.

For in their strength, lies true grace,
A testament to the human race.
Though trials may come, they stand tall,
The bravest hearts, the strongest thrall.

Authentic Kinship

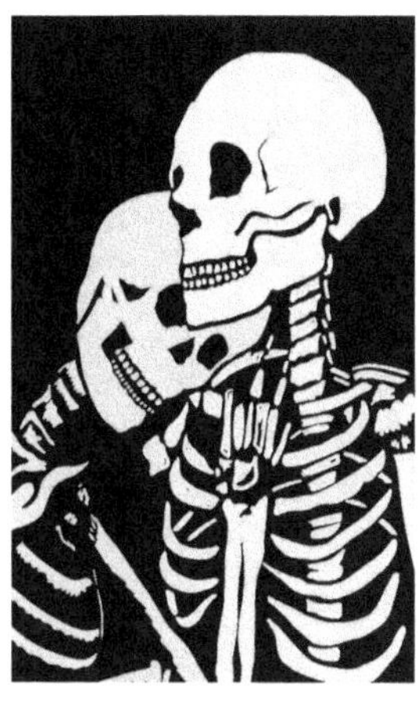

In the journey of healing, lessons unfold,
Honesty strengthens, never leaves you cold.
Speak your heart, let your feelings be known,
True connections deepen, seeds of trust sown.

Boundaries set, a sign of self-care,
Proper people respect, they're aware.
Authenticity shines, it's a priceless treasure,
Genuine bonds form, lasting beyond measure.

So learn from healing, embrace what it brings,
Honesty, boundaries, authenticity rings.
In this simple truth, find peace and growth,
For true connections, these lessons loathe.

Tomorrow's Perspective

In the hustle of today, we fret and fuss,
About things that seem to weigh on us.
But pause a moment, take a breath,
Consider this, before succumbing to stress.

A year from now, what seems so dire,
Will it still burn with the same fire?
The worries that keep us awake at night,
Might fade away in the morning light.

The troubles we face, both big and small,
Often lose their grip, their hold, their thrall.
For time has a way to rearrange,
Our worries, our fears, our emotional range.

So take heart, dear friend, and don't despair,
For burdens lighten with time to spare.
A year from now, you'll look back and see,
How fleeting these worries can truly be.

Let It Go!

In moments when life feels tangled and tight,
When questions haunt and days turn to night,
Remember, your peace is worth more, you
know,
Than unraveling mysteries and reasons to sow.

Let go of the need to always understand,
Sometimes life's course isn't what we planned.
Breathe deep, let the currents of worry subside,
Embrace the calm where true peace resides.

For in the quiet surrender, wisdom may bloom,
Letting go brings light where there once was gloom.
So cherish your peace, like a precious glow,
And let the reasons fade, let it all flow.

A Life Filled with Promises

In life, love blooms like a flower,
Bringing joy in every hour.
Peace whispers through the trees,
Calmly soothing all unease.

Healing hands mend broken parts,
Strengthening our hopeful hearts.
Progress paints the sky so bright,
Guiding us with steady light.

Blessings fall like gentle rain,
Washing away every pain.
Happiness in every smile,
Makes our journey all worthwhile.

Opportunity knocks each day,
Leading us along the way.
Life's canvas, a masterpiece,
Filled with hope that never leaves.

So cherish every moment true,
In this life that's meant for you.
With love, peace, and harmony,
A brighter future, let us see.

Wisdom's Way

In wisdom's realm, a truth is clear,
To correct a fool invites his ire,
But to the wise, a gift sincere,
A chance to learn, to grow, aspire.

A fool resents the light you shed,
His ego bruised, his pride unfed,
Yet wisdom blooms where minds are led,
To paths of truth, where hearts are wed.

So choose your words with gentle art,
For folly blinds, but wisdom starts
To build anew a thoughtful heart,
Where learning thrives, and grace imparts.

Beyond Expectations

Someday we'll find what we're searching for,
Or maybe we won't, that's unsure.
Perhaps we'll discover something grand,
Beyond what we dreamt, unplanned.

In quest of treasures, we may roam,
Through valleys deep, and fields unknown.
But life's true gifts, hidden in plain sight,
May bloom unexpectedly, pure and bright.

So cherish the journey, every twist and turn,
For what we seek, we may yet learn.
Not just the goal, but the path we tread,
Holds wonders and joys, by fate led.

For in the quest for our heart's desire,
We may find something even higher.
Embrace the unknown, with an open door,
Discovering riches we've yearned for, and more.

Cutting Out the Crap

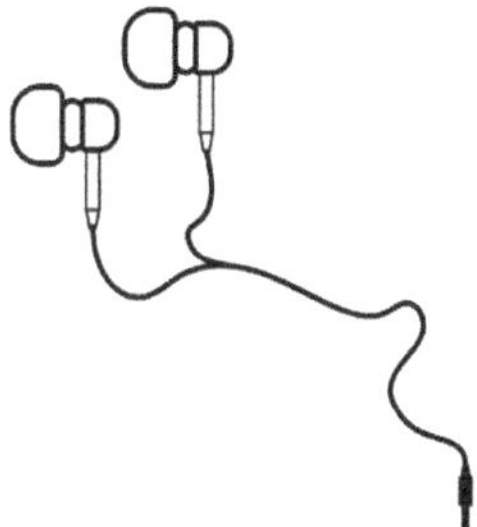

At your table, choose your chairs with care,
For some bring more trouble than flair.
Like dusting off ash from a cigarette,
Clear your life of those who bring regret.

Peaceful meals with laughter and cheer,
No room for negativity here.
Take out the chairs that spoil your feast,
Bid farewell to those who stir the least.

Life's too short for toxic games,
Remove the chairs with no good names.
Dust them off like ashes so light,
Make your world a place so bright.

So choose your chairs with utmost thought,
Let not negativity be sought.
Clear the space, make it pure,
Your table's set, of that be sure.

Blessings and Beyond!

From the universe, your dreams unfold,
Manifestations in your hands you hold.
But beyond mere wishes, it's wise to plead,
For discipline, to nurture what you need.

With wisdom, let blessings grow and thrive,
In the garden of life, keep dreams alive.
Motivation fuels the fire within,
To aim higher, and more dreams begin.

So ask of the universe, not just to receive,
But for the strength to believe and achieve.
With discipline, wisdom, and motivation true,
You'll see your dreams, and more, come through.

The Real Luxuries

As years go by, you start to see,
The luxuries that truly set you free.
Not diamonds bright or wealth untold,
But simple joys that soothe the soul.

A quiet morning, soft and slow,
Where time drifts by, a gentle flow.
With music soft, a calming tune,
That whispers secrets to the moon.

To choose your path, without constraint,
To savor moments without restraint.
These are the treasures, pure and true,
That age unveils, as life ensues.

So cherish time, embrace the slow,
Let melodies of peace bestow.
For in these luxuries, life is found,
In simple joys, forever profound.

Finding Home

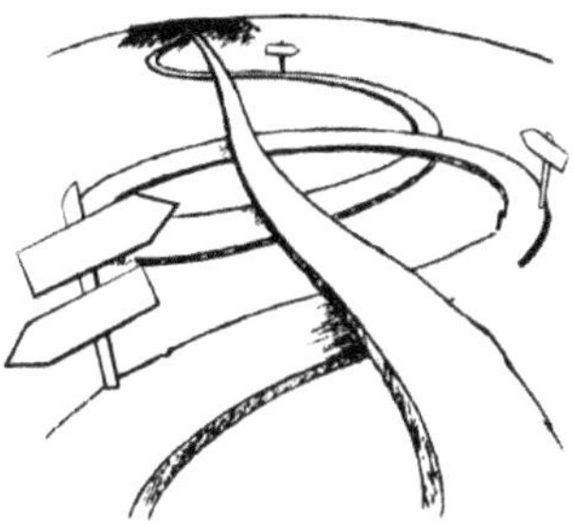

In the search for love, through tears and fears,
You gave your heart, through joy and tears.
To those who couldn't see your worth,
Yet you believed in love's rebirth.

But worry not, dear soul of mine,
For love will come, in its due time.
It travels far, through stars above,
To find its home in someone's love.

So hold on tight, and don't lose hope,
For destiny will help you cope.
The love you give will not be lost,
It finds its way, whatever the cost.

In someone's arms, you'll finally see,
A love that's true, a love that's free.
For all the love you thought was lost,
Has found its way, no matter the cost.

To all my readers, may you find,
A love that's gentle, pure, and kind.

The Invisible Clock

In the quiet moments, a clock does tick,
Unseen, unheard, it goes click by click.
Cherish the love that's given to thee,
For time slips away, as it's meant to be.

Hold close the ones who hold you near,
With laughter and joy, make memories dear.
Life's fleeting moments swiftly pass by,
So love with your heart, before they fly.

Though unseen, this clock won't stall,
Tick-tocking softly, reminding us all.
Embrace each day with all your might,
Love and be loved, in the morning light.

For time's steady march waits for none,
So dance in its rhythm, till the day is done.
Keep in mind this clock unseen,
Love, live, and cherish, in between.

Echoes of Pain

WAIT

In the quiet depths of restless hours,
Yearning whispers beg to be released,
Craving the melody of their voice,
Patience wanes, a fragile thread teased.
In the shadows of doubt, you confront,
Reasons elude, leaving you to abide,
Left suspended over time,
Yes, you wait, emotions amplified.

Waiting, a burden too heavy to bear,
Yet you endure, beyond what you should,
As they pass, indifferent, unchanged,
Still, you wait, in silent solitude.

Clutching hope in trembling hands,
A beacon against the endless gray,
For in the heart of uncertainty's fray,
Yes, you wait, for the dawn of a new day.

Yes, you wait!

Echoes of Solitude

In the depths of solitude, I wander lost,
Uncertain of the path ahead, the cost.
Yearning for someone, a guiding hand,
Yet solitude is all I understand.

Alone I tread through streets and squares,
In cafes, restaurants, I take my chairs.
Movies flicker on the silver screen,
But loneliness is all that I glean.

Work becomes my refuge, my escape,
Buying things to fill the void, a shape.
Yet the lies we tell ourselves, so deep,
As loneliness creeps in, we silently weep.

Calls from family, but they don't see,
The turmoil inside, the silent plea.
Emotions tangled, love turned sour,
In this bleak, desolate hour.

But I cling to hope, a flickering light,
Dreaming of a day, serene and bright.
When tears no longer stain my cheek,
And solitude's hold begins to peak.

For now, in the abyss, how do I flee?
With music, food, and drinks, yet no glee.
Searching for peace amidst the strife,
In this lonely dance, the rhythm of life.

Chasing Shadows

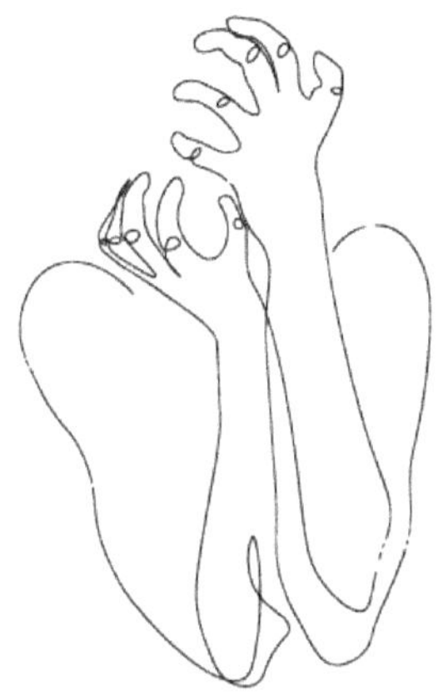

In the quiet of the night, your voice I hear,
A haunting melody, so crystal clear.
Memories of sweeter days gone by,
Echoes of laughter, now just a sigh.

We crafted dreams, mapped out our fate,
A journey to a better state.
But on that path, a stumble, a fall,
Leaving me wondering, why did you stall?

I stood by you in your darkest hour,
Through nights so bleak, I gave my power.
Yet when I needed you, where were you then?
Lost in the echoes, time and again.

Now I trace the map that leads me back,
To where our love was once on track.
But the roads you chose, they led astray,
Leaving me chasing shadows in dismay.

Your voice still lingers, I can't let go,
Caught in a dance, a bittersweet woe.
The map that leads to you, it draws me near,
Though I know now, you're no longer here.

I hear your voice in whispers so deep,
As I navigate this endless leap.
Yet I must move on, find a new way,
Away from the map that led astray.

Blinded by Trust and Love

In the realm of trust and love, a story unfolds,
Of friendship blooming, into love it molds.
But shadows lurked where honesty fades,
Deception hid in the sweet serenades.

We started as friends, then love took its place,
Yet unknown to me, I was just a second face.
Caught in a web where hearts entwine,
But truth unveiled, oh how love can blind.

Drama ensued, a stormy affair,
He went back, leaving me in despair.
Their reunion, as fleeting as ice in fire,
For his heart still burned with a different desire.

He returned, seeking a second chance,
Should I forgive? Or refuse this romance?
Blinded by trust, love's intricate dance,
I chose to give another shot, taking a chance.

Years have passed since that fateful day,
No more betrayals, yet pain found its way.
Taken for granted, my heartache profound,
In love's cruel game, I am forever bound.

To break free from this cycle, I strive and I cope,
But escaping love's grip feels beyond any hope.
Hurt, heartbroken, shattered, deprived,
In love's tangled web, I have often dived.

It's tough to break free from love's relentless
loop,
Where wounds run deep, and scars leave their
scoop.
Yet amidst the pain, a lesson I've found,
To cherish myself, on firmer ground.

For love may blind and love may deceive,
But strength in resilience, I will achieve.
No longer a victim of love's cruel art,
I'll heal, I'll rise, mending my heart.

Hazel and Anguish

In the days gone by, it all felt so right,
Underneath the stars, in your arms so tight.
I stood strong, believed in our song,
But now I'm adrift, where did we go wrong?

I can't breathe, nights without sleep,
Pieces of me shattered, buried deep.
Once whole, now torn apart by the lies,
Behind a smile, where my true self cries.

I trusted you with all, let you into my core,
You made me feel alive, like never before.
Now I'm a shadow, a ghost of who I was,
Broken-hearted because of our loss.

I blame myself for loving you too much,
Now I ache inside, longing for your touch.
But these tears I hide, they won't see the light,
Behind these hazel eyes, in the dark of night.

Swallowed by pain, spit out by fate's cruel game,
Loving you hurts, it's my heart you claim.
No more tears on my face, I hold them tight,
Broken yet standing, in the depths of night.

Here I stand, once more, in pieces I reside,
Can't deny this pain, can't run, can't hide.
Once believed you were my forever, my sun,
Now shattered dreams, where love once began.

But you won't see these tears I cry,
Behind these hazel eyes, where my feelings lie.

Here I am, once again,
Broken, but trying to mend.
Thought you were the one,
Now torn, deep inside,
Behind these hazel eyes, I hide.

In this turmoil, I find strength to face the day,
Though broken, I'll heal, find my own way.
For in these tears and in this pain,
I'll rise again, despite the rain.

Arsa Hua Kalam Uthaye

Kya kahu bahut dino se kuch likha nahi
Arsa hua kalam uthaye
Zindagi ki kashmakash aisi rahi pichle kuch din
Waqt hi nahi mila ki khud se hum ho muskuraye.

Dil aur dimag dono sath dete toh kuch bat bhi thi
Yahan toh na dil ka kuch pata tha
Dimag toh janab bhul hi jayein...
Mann tha adha khali adha bhara
Kabhi lafz na the, toh kabhi jazbaato ne hath
utha diye
Kabhi khechal kuch aisi rahi
Kabhi waqt aisa bhi tha jo na beet paye
Kya kahu janab, arsa hua kalam uthaye.

Givers and Takers

In the realm of friendships, I've faced a storm,
Giving much of myself, always in the norm.
Confiding in those I thought were true,
Yet they turned, betraying me out of the blue.

Bitter lessons learned from these so-called
friends,
Who chose deceit, where honesty ends.
Behind my back, they schemed and lied,
While I, unaware, trusted and tried.

Today's friends pretend, masks they wear,
But beneath the surface, they silently glare.
Jealous of my strides, my victories bright,
Gossiping tongues, they weave in the night.

Yet, I stand tall, believing in karma's embrace,
With actions and achievements, my path I trace.
Their jealousy burns, their souls shallow and
bare,
But I'll leave my mark, deep and dark, without a
care.

For true friendship's value, I've come to see,
Not in false smiles or deceitful glee.
In the end, karma's cycle will unfold,
As I rise strong, their envy will be told.

Love's Heavy Toll

My heart in pieces, shattered by you,
Broken repeatedly, through and through.
Always you, causing this pain,
Hurting me again and again.

Loving was supposed to be sweet,
But with you, it's a painful feat.
Being loved, an even tougher climb,
Leaves me here, alone in this time.

My chest aches, tears won't cease,
In this loneliness, seeking peace.
You don't ask, you don't care,
Leaving me in this despair.

What am I doing, I don't know,
Lost in emotions that won't show.
Confused, I stumble in this storm,
Waiting for understanding to form.

Amidst Petals and Pain

In life's tangled web, it's tough to thread
The ache, the oddity, the sorrow spread
Roses in hand, a solitary sight,
Yet in those moments, anguish takes flight.

Long has it been since roses graced my palm,
In their absence, loneliness's psalm.
With an old-fashioned heart, a romantic's woe,
Yearning for love's touch, in shadows to grow.

Lost not in confusion, but in the search
For what eludes me, an unreachable perch
Unable to grasp what my heart desires
Frustration mounts, stoking inner fires

Exhaustion weighs heavy, discontent profound
Yearning for love's touch, in silence drowned
Yet still, I carve through this desolate night
Longing for affection's warmth, craving its light.

Whispers of Redemption

Why do hearts betray?
Perhaps they tire of the familiar, grow weary of
routine,
Seeking new thrills, exploring the unknown,
Or simply find pleasure in the forbidden.

Yet, could it be they ache from neglect,
Longing for the tenderness they once knew?
Forgotten in the shadows, taken for granted,
Yearning for affection, for moments cherished.

In the labyrinth of emotion, lies tangled webs of
desire,

Where truth and temptation dance hand in hand.
But amidst the chaos, redemption may be found,
In the gentle touch of understanding,
In the vow to nurture what was once forsaken,
And in the dawn of a love reborn.

Manzar

Wo bhi ek manzar tha…
Ye bhi ek manzar hai,
Dil ki gehrayiyon mein jane
chubte kitne khanjar hai.

Wo bhi ek mahaul tha…
Ye bhi ek mahaul hai,
Anjaan hai log yahan sare
Tanhayiyan sabke andar hai.

Wo bhi ek waqt tha…
Ye bhi ek waqt hai,
Haste the jab sath mein sab
Aj sath baithte bhi nahi hai.

Wo bhi ek mukam tha…
Ye bhi ek mukam hai,
Unchayiyo par toh hain aj sab
Par koi kisi ke sath nahi hai.

Wo bhi ek ashiyaan tha
Ye bhi ek karvaan hai,
Wo Khushi ka ek jahan tha
Ye dukh ka ek asman hai.

Kehne ko toh bahut kuch hai
lafzo ki kami hamesha khalti hai,
dhundne toh niklte hai roz sham ko sukoon
Par dard ki subah bhi toh roz hoti hai.
Raat ka kya hai janaab…

raat ka… kya hai janaab,
ab sapne bhi nahi sirf neend hi ati hai
neend bhi mangti hai ab hisab…
puchti hai kaha gaye wo khwab,
unki yad bahut ati hai.

Khair chodiye, shayad ab kuch ho nahi sakta
shayad ab aur kuch kho nahi sakta
Wo bhi ek manzar tha…
Ye bhi ek manzar hai
is Dil ki gehrayiyon mein
chubte toh bahut se khanjar hai.

Rustic Emotions

In your darkest hour, do you call
In the name of your savior, standing tall?
Do you taste the bitterness of blame,
In moments tinged with greed and shame?

Implication and ill-will, they spread,
'Til sleep eludes you in your bed.
Amidst turmoil and impending doom,
Before the strike, before the gloom.

Feed the rain, my love, I plea,
Thirsty for your warmth, so free.
Dancing beneath passion's sky, we must,
In your love, I place my trust.

Avoiding failure is our game,
Yet true colors will bleed the same.
In misbehavior's fleeting embrace,
We find ourselves in this empty space.

I long for what comes after,
Where disaster can't shatter.
More than ever, I pray we stay,
Where 'enough' remains, come what may.

Feed the rain, my love, I plea,
Thirsty for your warmth, so free.
Dancing beneath passion's sky, we must,
In your love, I place my trust.

Don't walk away from this fire,
From the yearning of our desire.
When the world is burning, let's stay,
In this world turned to dust, find our way.

Feed the rain, my love, I plea,
Thirsty for your warmth, so free.
Dancing beneath passion's sky, we must,
In your love, I place my trust.

Don't walk away from our hearts' yearn,
In this world turned to dust, let's discern.

Come Find Me

We said our goodbyes, you and I,
But love's a game we cannot deny.
Like a river ever flowing,
You drift away, without me knowing.

Like a fire, always burning bright,
I'll wait here through the darkest night.
If you're ready, my heart's ajar,
Come find me, wherever you are.

Lost our way, you said last,
Through tears and shadows that have passed.
It took losing you to see,
Forever's search ends with me.

In the darkness, you're the light,
Guiding me through endless night.
If you're ready, my heart's a song,
Come find me, where you belong.

Run to me, don't ever stray,
In this dance, our hearts will play.
If you're ready, don't hesitate,
Come find me, it's never too late.

Actions Speak Louder

At the end of the day, it's crystal clear,
Who really cares and holds you dear.
It's not just words or promises grand,
But how they act, where hearts truly stand.

Do they consider how you feel,
And make sure their actions heal?
Or do they cause you pain and strife,
With every careless move in life?

True care's not shown in words alone,
But in every action, thoughtfully shown.
If they treasure your heart, it will show,
In every step, they'll let you know.

So, worry not about what they say,
But watch their deeds along the way.
For those who truly want to stay,
Their caring actions will light the way.

Big Heart's Curse

Having a big heart, what a curse, oh dear,
People mistake kindness for being naive, I fear.
Cut them off, they still point the blame,
For their own faults, what a shame.

Big heart, big problem, so they say,
But who's the fool at the end of the day?
Kindness mistaken, intelligence doubted,
Cut them off, their accusations shouted.

So here's to big hearts, misunderstood and
bright,
Keep cutting off those who can't see the light.
Blame me once, shame on you,
Blame me twice, well, that's nothing new.

Could Have, Should Have!

Don't stress the could haves, they say,
For if they should have, they'd find a way.
Coulda, woulda, shoulda, the trio's in play,
But reality's not fond of delay.

If it were meant to be, it'd unfold,
No need for regrets, stories untold.
Should have been clearer, they'd sigh,
But fate's not known for being shy.

Could have been roses, could have been gold,
Could have been legends, stories so bold.
But here we are, in the realm of would,
Where could haves fade, as they should.

So let go of the could haves, bid them adieu,
What should have been, it would be true.

In the land of ifs, we'll settle and stay,
For what should have, it would find its way.

Beyond the Pain

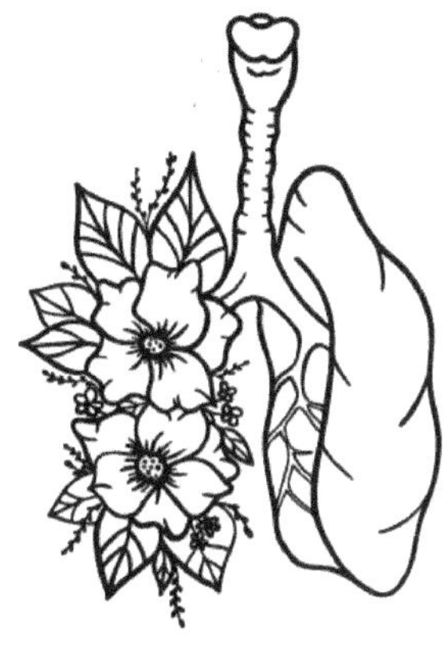

In the depths where shadows creep,
Lies a peace so still, so deep.
But to reach that tranquil shore,
One must brave the tempest's roar.

Across the waves of sorrow's sea,
Where pain's relentless, wild and free,
The heart finds solace, calm, and grace,
In the quietude of a healing embrace.

Though fears may whisper, doubts may reel,
Strength arises from wounds that heal.
For the peace you seek, serene and real,
Is found beyond the pain you feel.

So tread bravely through the darkest night,
Know each step brings you to the light.
For in the struggles, trials, and rain,
Lies the path to peace, beyond the pain.

Family Chronicles

FAMILY

We are family,
We might not resemble,
Certainly, we don't dress alike…
I am black and you are white.
We might not settle on the same things,
Yes, we argue, yes, we fight.
Yes, we share a lot of things,
From times of sorrow to times of light.
Pictures hanging there might get old,
But the memories that we share
They are always going to stay strong and bold.

Yes, we are family,
We might not resemble,
Certainly, we don't dress alike…
Yes, we argue, yes, we fight.
No matter what the differences are
but... yes, there is something
Something that holds us together,
Love, memories, our bond, and compassion
Family we are, now and forever.

Beautiful Roses

A word is written… and chapters are closed,
Memories come across… and again, the old
wind blows,
You share your life with people
However, time comes and goes.
They say time heals everything.
But an arrow, once left, never returns to its bow.

When I dive into the depths of time,
I see a strong pillar, a pillar as strong as the
spine.
I see in the very smooth days,
I was waking up to warm mornings

Following the probable monotonous regime
But then comes a day when you are struck by
surprise
Like the silence before the storm
Like something terrible in an innocent disguise.

When I dive into the depths of time,
My memories take me back
To a day so pure and fine;
A sunny Friday, nothing quite new,
A cold evening and dinner on time.
It was a basic family Friday,
All of us sitting together, sharing random laughs
and smiles.

Dinner was done; it was then time to rest
Went into my room and lying on the bed
Reading a book; hardly did I realize
I dozed off on the pile of blankets on my side.
The lights were on, but my consciousness was
gone.
It was midnight, then he entered
Woke me up slightly,
Tucked me in bed as cultured.
He lay the blanket on me
And switched off the lights,
There I went into deep sleep
Everything was oh so right.

The following day, it was half past five
Hardly was I awake; I heard them
They said that he was not well and upright.
Everyone suggested he should rest
He wanted to go to work,
He simply didn't ever like to prioritize his
health.
Forcing him to take some rest
He said, "Don't disturb me then or come into my
room
Cause I want to rest properly
So that I can go to work at noon."

Mom went to him after some time
"Do you need anything?"
And he said, "I am fine."
After a few hours, she went again
But there came no response, this time…

We shrugged and moved him
No expression on his wrinkled face
There was no breath
His hands lay there lifeless.
At that moment came the realization
Things will never stay the same furthermore
At that moment, emotions rushed
As my Grandpa was not there with us anymore.

I dive into the depth of time,

And I am taken back to the moment
When he laid the blanket on the back of mine
I am taken back to all the shared moments
And memories flood back as tears in my eyes
Yes, it isn't that long ago
A Saturday morning on November 29
You were the one with the greatest cheers,
You were the family's spine.

Today, your memories are the only things we are
left with!
I won't say that I miss you,
Because it is much deeper than what I'll always
cherish.
The memories of your smile,
The endless conversations we used to have at
night,
How you used to place your hand on my head
How your guidance would make everything
right.
The tear-filled eye then closes,
Like our family is the garden,
And your memories are the
beautiful roses.

Greed's Tempest

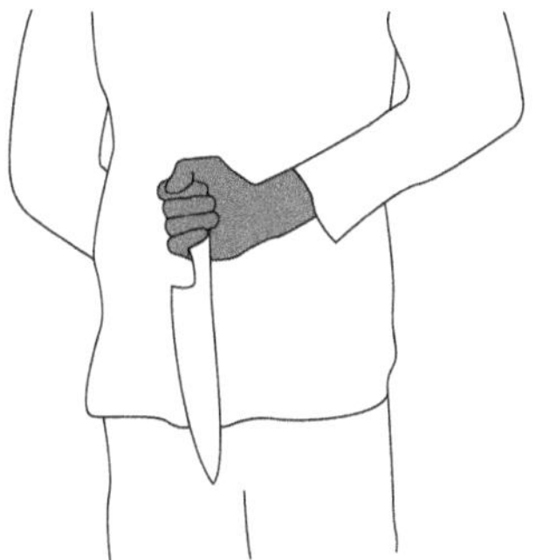

In life's relentless race, we chase elusive days,
Seeking fortune's foresight in a world of maze.

Strange, how greed consumes, for coins and
gold we pine,
Obsessed with others' wealth, covetous hearts
entwine.

Among us lurk such souls, hungry for what's not
theirs,
They measure worth in riches, their envy wears
no airs.

They covet without earning, desire without
strive,
Their thirst for wealth unquenched, in a
ceaseless drive.

They grasp at gold and cars, dowries and cash in
hand,
Yet their insatiable hunger, like shifting sand.

In grief's tender embrace, they seek profit's gain,
No solace in loss, their motives darkly stain.

They quarrel at gravesides, devoid of empathy's
grace,
For in their world of greed, respect finds no
place.

They barter peace for the coin, manipulate and
deceive,
In their quest for wealth, and humanity they
bereave.

Amidst the ashes of virtue, they stand tall,
Blind to the bonds of kinship, they heed no call.

But judgment falls not upon us, mere players in
fate's scheme,
For karma whispers truths, in life's intricate
dream.

When It All Falls Down

In a world gone astray, in a world so wild,
Where every heartache seems like a trial,
We stand strong, just you and I,
Facing the storm, under the same sky.

When darkness falls and fear takes flight,
I'll be your beacon, shining bright.
Through the chaos, we'll find our way,
Two souls together, come what may.

They say it's tough, this road we tread,
But with you, Dad, I'm not misled.
In a ghost town of doubts, we'll build anew,
Love our foundation, strong and true.

Hold my hand, don't let go,
In this mad world, we'll make it so.
When it all falls, when it all falls down,
We'll be the light, no longer bound.

For in your arms, I find my cover,
In your love, I discover
Strength to face whatever may come,
Together, Dad, we'll overcome.

So let's sing our song, like Madonna's tune,
Through the darkness, beneath the moon.
No matter how cold this world may be,
You and I, forever free.

When it all unravels, when the world's a haze,
We'll be two souls in this labyrinthine maze,
Hand in hand, through the shadows we'll roam,
Together we'll find our way back home.

When it all crumbles, when it all falls apart,
We'll be two souls with a beating heart,
Side by side, through thick and thin,
Together, forever, never apart
So let the journey begin.

I HAVE TO GO

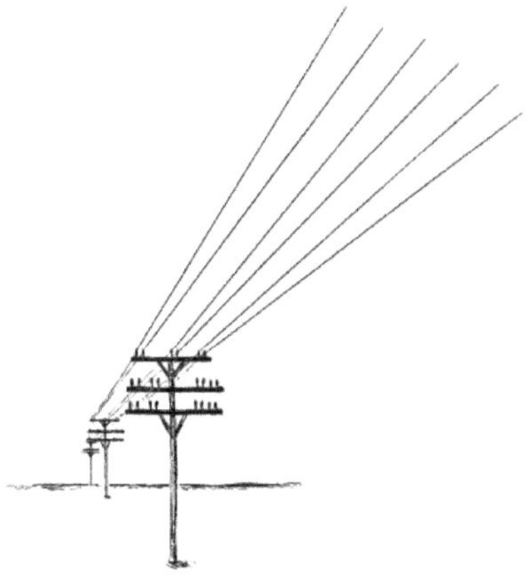

I know you don't want me to go,
It hurts, it is agonizing
And yes, it is difficult,
But… I have to leave
Please let me go.

I know for me you had different plans,
A completely different time and life
A completely different trance.

Time gains pace,
Things and people change with time,
You and I have changed
Who thought… growing up could be such a
crime?

The memories aren't old
When your hands held mine
Your strength still makes me strong and bold.
I have always loved your everything… your
love, your anger
Your denials, your behavior turned cold,
But your sadness, oh! It makes me cry.

I know you are not happy, neither am I
All I need is your hands to hold mine…
For you to tell me that you got my back,
Probably a hug, and I'll be just fine.

I know how you hide your sadness,
Your anger becomes a disguise.
I know how you lie and not sleep…
Sleep is also deprived of my eyes.

I haven't ever expressed my love for you,
I never do… it is endless, it is something I can't
explain
And certainly, no lines are enough,
No words can make it through.

The reticent relationship that we share,
Neither do you express… nor do I.
But dear Dad, your daughter always knows,
Of everything that you hide.

I know I am someone very stubborn,
Someone very reckless and rebel
But this rebel devil of yours loves you more than
you'll ever know,
More than you can ever tell.

Yes,
I have to go…
Yes, it is painful, it hurts
It is agonizing; And yes, it is difficult…
But Paa, please know,
Deep down, I also don't want to leave
I also don't want to go.

Swagger Serenades

A Roar Obscure

In silence, I once held my fears tight,
Afraid to stir the waters, afraid of the fight.
Quietly I nodded, agreed in compliance,
Forgot my voice, forgot my defiance.

You pushed me, tested me, beyond what I could
bear,
I stood for nothing, I was caught in despair.
But you can't hold me down, I rise from the dust,
I found my voice, I found my trust.

You hear me now, hear my thunderous cry,
I'll shake the ground, reach for the sky.
From being held back, I've had enough,
I see clearly now, I'm strong and tough.

With the eye of the tiger, I'm a fighter bold,
Through flames I dance, my story unfolds.
A champion's heart beats within my core,
You'll hear me roar, louder than before.

Like a butterfly, I float and weave,
Swift as the wind, I fiercely believe.
From nothing to everything, my journey's clear,
I'm my own hero, shedding every fear.

So hear me roar, like a lioness proud,
Through trials and triumphs, my voice is loud.
I am a champion, this truth I'll restore,
You're gonna hear me roar, forevermore.

Strings of Deception

I dance with a narcissist, hearts in a twist,
Yet they're drawn to me like my violin's sweet tryst.
I play them well, each move a choreographed play,
For every lie spun, they offer me more in a sway.

The world spins thus, his thoughts swirl around me,
A blaze caresses my skin, crimson hues set free.
With painted lips and unshaken will,
I owe them naught, for they had their fill.

"They claim I've done wrong," they cry in vain,
Yet why does it feel so justified, the pleasure not feigned?

The thrill of it all, the rush like no other,
A symphony of mischief, a secret to smother.

I never trust a playboy, yet they flock near,
Across the globe, they follow, guided by fear.
I let them believe they rescued me, a twist of
fate,
But before they know it, it's too late.

The blaze licks higher, whispers abound,
"Never squander a treasure," they say,
spellbound.
But if they dare cross my name in vain,
Their reckoning's due, just like the rain.

"They claim I've done wrong," the world's
refrain,
Yet why does it thrill me, casting aside pain?
The joy of the game, the rush of the chase,
Over and over, a smile on my face.

They burn all the witches, though I'm no such
thing,
With their proof and their pitchforks, my heart's
on a string.
So ignite the flames, let them blaze bright,
For I'll dance in its glow, unafraid in the night.

"They claim I've done wrong," echoes loud,
Yet why does it feel so justified amidst the
crowd?
The thrill of the game, the pleasure so true,
A paradox lived, a tale overdue.

Oh, they say I did something terrible, they say
with a sneer,
But why does it feel so good, the rush so dear?
In the dark of the night, in the shadows, I roam,
My violin's strings, in my heart, find their home.

Shadows of Doubt

Silence
How profound is the silence of this night,
Yet it brings no solace, only unrest...
So many questions, so many answers, so many
dreams,
Incomplete they are, lost in the shadows of
doubt.

Within me lies an incompleteness... perhaps!
My mind feels hollow...
Is it just the nature of time? Perhaps!
Why does no one stand by me, ever?

Is it just the nature of time?
Or a consequence of circumstance...
Will anything ever be set right?
But let that be a tale for another time!

I ponder how different things could have been...
I ponder how different they still might be;
But here I stand, searching for my destination...
I ponder, could this path have been any
different?

I ponder, whom should I blame as the culprit?
Neither time stood by me, nor did my loved
ones.
There's an emptiness in my heart...
But whom should I blame as the culprit?
Neither time stood by me, nor did my loved
ones.

Years have passed, spent in constant struggle,
Now, I am weary...
Years have passed, endured with patience,
But now, I am weary.

I am weary now...
Yet there's still much to do,
Yes! I am weary...
But there's still much to fight for,
Time has never been forgiving...

Even now, it remains unforgiving,
Should I pause? Take a moment to breathe?
But no, there's still a long journey ahead!

This time is peculiar indeed,
Here, one must fight even for their rights...
But what use is a right for which one must fight,
After all, rights are meant to be received from
rights!

Broken Grace

In the whispers of your thoughts, I roam,
In your glittering prime, but not alone.
Sparkling lights, a facade they create,
Concealing the turmoil, the inner debate.

They say, "Fake it till you make it," they insist,
So you smile, though inside you resist.
A tough kid, they label you strong,
Yet inside, you feel everything's wrong.

Promises made, love pledged for life,
But time cuts short, causing strife.
Pieces of you scattered on the floor,
Yet you keep performing, wanting more.

Every day feels like a birthday cheer,
Yet tears flow, but productivity's near.
You cry a lot, but you still strive,
An art born from pain, to survive.

You hold your breath, searching for clues,
In drawers, finding remnants you can use.
Confident you'll pass this test,
Through tears, you still give your best.

You're good, so good, though they may not see,
The hidden battles, the silent plea.
But in your brokenness, you find your art,
Mastering life's stage, with a brave heart.

Ode to Moving On

On a rainy day, you were gone, oh what a thrill,
I smashed my violin and set fire to your room,
just for the chill.
Your stuff in the ocean, a bag's perfect potion,
Watched it sink, no emotion, like a true
devotion.

You're on one road, I'm in the Sombrero's
expanse,
Earthbound you want me, but I'm lost in cosmic
dance.
So hard to please, your outdated stance,
You're stuck in the '70s, I'm a '90s romance.

I don't care, I love it, your drama so fine,
But honey, your retro style ain't on my timeline.
So let's kill this switch, let go of the past's hitch,
Your backward thinking, darling, belongs in a
ditch.

I love it, I love it, this sarcastic delight,
Moving on to the future, leaving you in
hindsight.

Rebel Reflections

Easier said than done: "When desires burn fierce
and bright,
Break the chains of rules, and let your spirit take
flight.
Forget the limits, stereotypes, and traditions that
bind,
Embrace your dreams wholeheartedly, leave
doubts behind."

In a world brimming with myriad hues,
Strange it seems, individuals will not enthuse.
Careers, choices, decisions, initially scorned,
In a world that's progressed, norms still adorned.

Ah, imagination, a potent force, indeed,
Weaving realms where aspirations freely breed.
Yet reality's harsh truths often quench the flame,
Leaving us in a world far from the dream's
acclaim.

This isn't just about you or me,
But those aspirations are broken, can't you see?
Those dreams, once within grasp, are now adrift,
Aiming high, yet reality's rift.

At birth, parents pave the way,
With dreams for the child, come what may.
But when the time beckons for choices to be
made,
Whose voice, whose dreams, shall aid?

Perspectives vary, conflicting views arise,
Whose dream to pursue, whose vision to prize?
Communication, understanding, the bridge to
mend,
Parent and child, on aspirations, to blend.

Yet, alas, my reality took another path,
Guided not by my heart's own aftermath.
A surgeon's dream, a childhood aim,
Redirected, altered, not quite the same.

Commerce, a realm I didn't seek,
Yet forced to tread, my spirit weak.
Tenth standard's innocence, a fragile state,
Bound by choices, sealed by fate.

Two years of apathy, of disinterest's plight,
Studying aimlessly, devoid of light.
Pressure mounting, expectations tall,
A soul adrift, amidst the fall.

Nights of stress, sleepless tears,
Marks and scores, engulfing fears.
No guidance, no solace, in sight,
A rebel's seed, taking flight.

Stereotypes loom, Indian parents' decree,
Mental turmoil, a silent plea.
Misunderstood, the struggles faced,
Beneath the facade, emotions are encased.

Board exams, a final stand,
Praying silently, for a passing hand.
Acceptance sought, in modest grades,
Yet scorned, for marks that fade.

Confidence waned, self-esteem bruised,
Pretense worn, emotions diffused.
Beneath the mask, a soul aflame,
Rebel rising, against the blame.

Amidst the chaos, amidst the strife,
The rebel within, claims its life.
No regrets, no shame, in the fight,
For against injustice, stands the light.

Though labeled rebel, devil's child,
Proudly standing, free, and wild.
Against norms and traditions, dare to strive,
In the rebel's anthem, truly alive.

Defying Hypocrisy

In the tides of time, I found a tome of old,
Where ink had etched the truths my heart did hold.
"Change," it whispered, "is the only constant sway,
Yet some in darkness deem it as foul play.

In the halls of wisdom, where fools parade,
Men cloak themselves, in wisdom's charade.
They claim the mantle, the sons of the line,
Yet wield their words like a poisoned vine.

Their kin, they abuse with a cruel hand,
Their minds are shackled by greed's demand.
They covet a son, an heir to their name,
While daughters they cast into shadows of
shame.

But the fault lies not in gender's decree,
It festers within their twisted ideology.
Women too, with hearts as cold as stone,
Spew venom upon their sisters, unknown.

They clutch at power, with greedy claws,
Their hearts are untouched by mercy's laws.
They weave a web of lies and deceit,
Their tongues dripping honey, yet venom
replete.

But fear not the darkness that they weave,
For in their shadows, you shall not grieve.
Stand tall, against their toxic sway,
For truth shall dawn upon the darkest day.

You cannot sever ties that bind,
But in your heart, the peace you'll find.
They spread their poison, their venomous seed,
But in your strength, you shall be freed.

For it is the rebel within, the sane voice,
That cries out against their vile choice.

With courage as your sword, and truth your
guide,
You'll vanquish the darkness, with hearts untied.

And as I turn the page, with tear-stained eyes,
I see the truth, beneath their lies.
For in my battles, I've found my pride,
Against the currents, I've dared to stride.

So let the ink flow, let the words dance,
For in their rhythm, I find my chance.
To rise above, to break free,
And live my life, unbound and free.

FIGHT

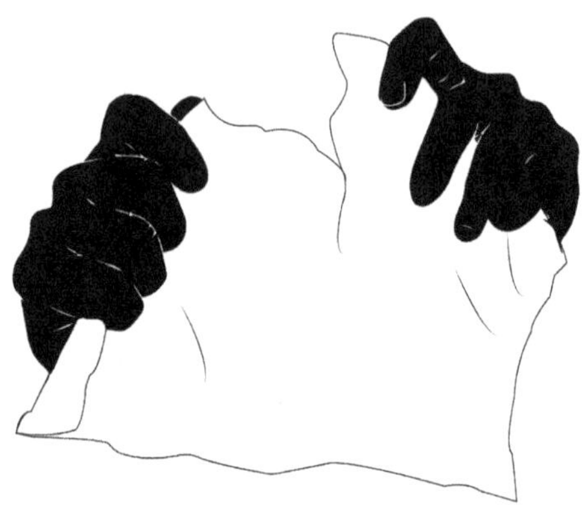

It's a strange thing about life,
You don't get anything without a fight.
You set your goals and aspirations
But the "jealous" always try to bring you down,
You want to head high with your inspirations
But they take your morale down.

There is never going to be a lack of such
All you've got to do is keep moving,
Without a demotivated hunch.
You have to fight with everyone out there,
With the ones who don't believe in you
With those who envy you
With those who want you to react and care
The list is endless

Keep your eyes wide open, especially for the
unfair.
The sugar coaters are never to trust
Your success and happiness are their failures
They want you to fail; for them, your suffering is
a must.

They can be anyone
The stereotypes, the society, the culture,
Even the ones in your bloodline
They are the most toxic
And won't ever wish for your any good or fine.

They try and break you
They don't like the good in you
But this isn't about me or you,
It is about those broken aspirations that may
wound you.

A day might come when
You start reaching your saturation point
A point where your frustration can't be
controlled
You might start acting out,
And your anger cannot be contained in you
anymore.

You might fall, but you'll have to get up on your
own,

There might be nobody to hold your hand to
pick you up,
You might get bruised and badly hurt
But accept your scars, grow stronger and get up.
It is after that that you'll have no fear,
It was from then that you'll fight for everything
unfair.

If after everything from which you have suffered
You are declared to be the rebel,
I'd suggest don't you care,
Bow unto blame, and for less don't you ever
settle.

Harmony Amidst Turmoil

In the depths of silent nights, I ponder,
Why do my words dissolve, like mist in dawn's
wonder?
In a world where ears are deaf to my plea,
Why does my truth drift, untethered and free?

Why must the horizon of minds be so narrow?
In a realm where openness seems to be in
shadow.
Why must I wage wars, for my beliefs to thrive,
With those I hold dear, for whom I strive?

Why is love a battlefield, where scars we bear?
Why must I fight for the right to care?
Haven't I sowed kindness, in fields of my deeds?

Why do I reap discord, from these scattered
seeds?

When will the clouds part, and clarity shine?
When will I reclaim this essence of mine?
In a world so suffused with toxic air,
I yearn for the breeze of solace, fair.

May the tides of time wash away this strife,
And bring forth a dawn, with promise rife.
In the whispers of hopeful dreams,
I seek refuge from life's turbulent streams.

Let me break free from these chains unseen,
To wander in realms where my spirit can glean.
Grant me the serenity to rise above,
And find solace in the warmth of love.

So, I'll hold on to hope, amidst the fray,
Believing that brighter tomorrows pave the way.
For in the tapestry of life, woven with care,
There lies a thread of hope, beyond despair.

Resilience Forged

In the crucible of life, I've forged my path,
Hustling through years, facing tempests' wrath.
In those early days, battles fierce and stark,
Struggling for independence, light in the dark.

Loved ones doubted, questioned my aim,
But I fought for my dreams, stoked my own
flame.
Tears were shed, nights were long,
Yet I stood resilient, steadfast and strong.

Each day a skirmish, each victory small,
Building a career, scaling every wall.
I've cried, I've manipulated, I've fought,
Yet through it all, my determination wrought.

Now I stand amidst the fruits of my grind,
A testament to resilience, heart, and mind.
Life's not easy, nor handed on a platter,
But with my head held high, I've only grown
fatter.

Not in riches, but in wisdom and grit,
I'll keep pushing forward, never to quit.
For the fight's not over, challenges anew,
I'm ready, I'm hungry, to see this through.

No obstacle too daunting, no foe too strong,
I'll hustle, I'll fight, where I belong.
In the arena of life, I stake my claim,
To rise, to conquer, to never be tamed.

Rising Above!

Once they walked away, feeling small and
bereft,
But little did they know, it was just the first step.
Through tears and pain, through the darkest of
nights,
They found their own way back into the light.

With each dawn that broke, a new strength was
found,
In the quiet moments, in the footsteps on solid
ground.
They learned to smile again, with a heart that
grew strong,
Proving to themselves that they truly belong.

They built a life full of laughter and grace,
Filling the void left by their absence and space.
No longer defined by the hurt of the past,
But by the love they found, and the peace that
will last.

For the best revenge, they finally see,
Is the joy of becoming who they were meant to
be.
Their life shines brighter now, for all to behold,
A testament to resilience, a story retold.

Guardian of Peace

In the quiet depths of my soul,
I stitched together piece by piece,
A universe of peace and whole,
Where joy and calm would never cease.

Through storms that tore and winds that blew,
I labored on with grit and grace,
Rebuilding all I thought I knew,
In this sacred, sheltered space.

Now guarded like a precious gem,
My heart's door is not flung wide,
For those who seek to enter them,
Must prove their love, not just abide.

So if you wonder why I'm choosy,
In whom I let my light shine through,
It's because I've toiled long and mousy,
To find this peace I hold so true.

Autonomous Spirit

In the quiet strength of her stride,
A woman stands with quiet pride,
She shuns the need to ask or borrow,
Her spirit, steadfast, knows no sorrow.

With every penny earned and spent,
Her independence, a testament,
To strength that's born from deep within,
A heart that's proud, a will akin.

She holds her secrets close, you see,
Her money's path is hers to be,
For leaning on another's hand,
Is not the way she's made to stand.

A Capricorn's determined soul,
Whose spirit knows its steadfast goal,
To forge a path with will so strong,
In silence, she will prove her song.

So watch her as she walks her way,
Through nights and into brighter days,
For in her quiet, sturdy stance,
She finds her power, her own dance.

Mountain Strong: Ode to a Capricorn Woman

In the heart of the mountain, she stands strong
and tall,
A Capricorn woman, determined through it all.
With plans as precise as the stars in the sky,
She maps out her dreams, never questioning
why.

Her exterior tough, her spirit profound,
Yet beneath lies a softness, rarely unbound.
She hides her affection, but it's there, you'll see,
For those she holds dear, like you and like me.

From melancholy brooding to laughter's bright
gleam,
Her humor is dry, her wit like a stream.
In love, she's a romantic, though she may not
show,
Planning futures together before you even know.

At home, she's a queen, in control of her space,
With antiques and memories, time can't erase.
She's meticulous, tidy, with a spot for each thing,
In the warmth of her hearth, her true self takes
wing.

In her career, she's a force, climbing higher each
day,
Driven by ambition, come what may.
With a work ethic unmatched, she strives for her
best,
In her own business domain, she finds true zest.

So here's to the Capricorn, steadfast and true,
A powerhouse woman, through and through.
With a heart full of dreams and a spirit of grace,
She conquers her world, at her own steady pace.

Dreams Woven: A Symphony of Aspirations

In the tapestry of life, I weave my dreams,
A symphony of aspirations, in gentle streams.
To learn, to grow, in work's embrace,
And dance with skills, in career's chase.

To sculpt my form, both body and mind,
A canvas of health, in hues refined.
I'll shed the weight of yesterday's plight,
And dawn a visage, glowing and bright.

With every step, I'll paint a smile,
On faces dear, across the mile.
For family's joy, my heart's decree,
To nurture bonds, and set them free.

In love's sweet arms, I'll find my rest,
With vows exchanged, we'll be truly blessed.
A haven of love, where dreams unite,
In harmonious bliss, through day and night.

A nest of comfort, draped in delight,
A sanctuary where dreams take flight.
In luxury's embrace, I'll find reprieve,
Where joy resides and sorrows leave.

Adventures beckon, in daring's call,
To taste the thrill, and stand tall.
In life's grand tapestry, I'll leave my mark,
A legacy of joy, through light and dark.

With open arms, I'll greet the new,
In lands uncharted, and skies of blue.
To walk the paths, where history lies,
And unravel tales beneath the skies.

With faith as my compass, and hope as my
guide,
I'll manifest dreams, with nothing to hide.
For in this journey, I'll seize the day,
And watch my desires, come what may.

Let the whole world burn!

In the rush of the highway's song,
Where speed and light belong,
Through the air, I scream and fly,
Into the night, aiming high.

Restless heart, it's time to roam,
Leaving behind my old home.
Tomorrow's mystery unfolds bright,
Past's blurry lines fade in the night.

Injustice, if ever in my name,
I accept it and take the blame.
Give me all I need, my dear,
Love me till the morning's here.

Set the world ablaze, let it burn,
With desire's bitter-sweet yearn.
Chase away the shadows deep,
Let oblivion and peace in; let me sleep.

Drifting like a lost ship's tale,
In shadows where echoes prevail.
Longing for a distant shore,
Where love's embrace awaits once more.

Give me all I need, my dear,
Love me till the morning's here.

Set the world ablaze, let it burn,
With desire's bitter-sweet yearn.
Chase away the shadows deep,
Let oblivion and peace in; let me sleep.

Have you felt love's fiery sun?
Reason enough why I still run.
Disappear into neon's glare,
Give me all I need, my love to share.

Set the world ablaze, let it burn,
With desire's bitter-sweet yearn.
Chase away the shadows deep,
Let oblivion and peace in; let me sleep.

Beware the Enchantress

In the realm where magic weaves its course,
Beware the enchantress with a force.
She's sweet temptation, a spell to heed,
But tread lightly, for she takes the lead.

With eyes that lure like Cytherea's grace,
She beckons you into her embrace.
A perfect storm, she's bound to be,
Once you're hers, you're never free.

Her love, a drug, so strong and deep,
It pulls you in, no chance to keep
Your heart intact, if you dare to play,
With the enchantress who leads astray.

A roller coaster ride through the night,
She'll mesmerize with all her might.
But know, dear heart, before you fall,
She'll leave you enchanted, standing tall.

So heed these words, oh daring soul,
When faced with magic, stay in control.
For once you choose to dance this course,
Beware the power of the enchantress's force.

The Fence and the Ax

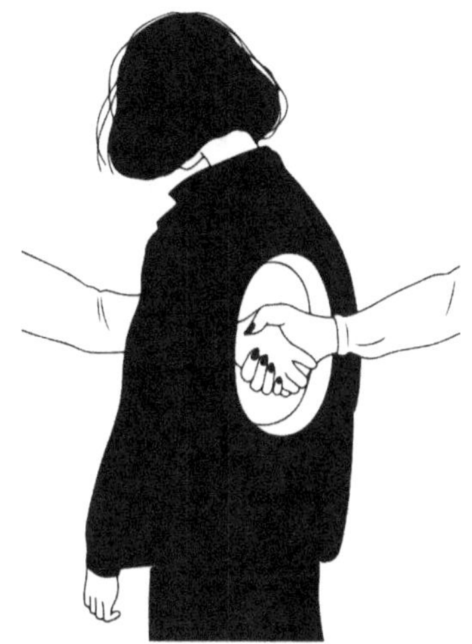

In the midst of laughter, in the glow of the night,
We swam in love's ocean, everything felt so
right.
No rules could bind us, no fences in our way,
Just the rhythm of our hearts, like a Gatsby
soirée.

But you came with storms, raining on my
parade,
Shaking my trust, leaving me dismayed.
Had to lock the gates, bid the niceties adieu,
Because of all the hurtful things you put me
through.

I gave you chances, like friends do, with grace,
Yet you twisted words, threw them in my face.
I took an axe to fences, once again broken,
Realizing your deception, words left unspoken.

Here's to my true friends, who stood by my side,
Through the whispers and drama, they never did
hide.
Here's to my dad, whose love knows no bounds,
And to my sister, for hearing my heart's sounds.

And here's to forgiveness, though it's hard to
find,
For this is why we can't have nice things, in my
mind.
You broke them, you shattered, the trust we once
knew,
This is why we can't have nice things—thanks to
you.

Red Underlined

I dislike your childish games,
Your stage, forever bent.
You cast me as the foolish pawn,
No, you, I don't commend.

I dislike your flawless schemes,
How you chuckle at each lie.
You claimed the blame was mine to bear,
Not cool, not at all, not I.

But I grew wiser, grew tougher just in time,
Like a phoenix, I rise, reborn from the grime.
I keep a tally of names, yours etched in crimson,
Checked it once, then twice, in my crown.

Oh, see what you forced me to pursue,
See the changes I've gone through.

I don't trust a soul, no one trusts me,
The actress in your nightmares, that's me.

Now watch what you made me do,
What you've forced me into.
Sorry, you'll never find the sweet, old me,
Why? She's gone, that's the fee.

Oh, so scrutinize what you made me do,
See the person I've become, it's true.

Love's Whispers

Coming Back Home

Time is hilarious and absurd
It takes you to roller coasters
Without any reason or word,
Strange things happen
To all flocks and herds.

Stories of hatred and love are formed of all old
and new
Some tales are forgotten…
Some stay forever anew
Similar is a story…
The story of these two…
The tale is probably possessed by very few.

It all started from being the very strangers
To the confusion between friendship and
attraction,

The bond which had hidden sparks and wonders
The bond very soon leads to never-ending
affection.
The affection that none of them could behold
The affection that someday had to burst out
With no sign of what time will hold.

And yes… it came… the time came
The time for the broken pieces to get back
together
For the bond which probably none of them had
ever.
Unknowingly the orbits narrowed between the
two
And certainly, none of them could have been
blamed
Ans yes… it happened… 'they' happened.

Amongst the silly funny talks…
Amongst the aimless useless walks,
They came together,
With no thought in mind
With no expectations from time
They came with some feelings...
The feelings which were so undefined.

Things began unexpectedly
Time moved according to its pace,
Slowly both fell... for each other's grace

Hardly did they know what time had in store
Separations had to surely happen
And this truth was so sore.

Finally, the difficult day came
"He had to go. But hardly did it affect 'Them'
Schedules changed and priorities as well…
He became so assiduous
While she was probably going through hell.

Days and months passed
Until then the day of the test came...
"I want to end Us firmly said 'He'
After hearing this... so broken she became,
'She' pleaded as hard as she could
'She' was on the grounds and beseeched more
than she should.
Hardly was he affected and remained in crusts
She asked for reasons...
But ah! He didn't have any,
Only she was at stake on her trusts.

Situations didn't change for days,
Her intuition kept waiting for the 'twist' in her
ways;
Disguised reasons and excuses were given to her
The truth was... the lie that he was hiding
But yeah! Things can't hide for too long they
say.

Her heart was not broken in haste,
But was being cut into pieces each day.
Hollow was she from inside...
But the last candle had to blow off
Till she actually opened her eyes.

She was 'bluffed' was what she saw
Everything she had and felt till then became
meaningless
Questions and memories crossed her mind with
aw;
So broken was she... everything for her became
worthless,
She asked him 'Why?' To which probably he
didn't have any answer
Things ended but something... somewhere was
left,
Something that needed to be fixed
But was so unkempt.

She made up her mind... not to go that way,
Cause she saw already how much he should
have
And how much he stayed.
'Sorry' is just a word
When someone is hurt, it just can't heal the
wounds
Time passed but never gained pace

Then something happened
Which proved to be the Ace of Spades!

'He' came back home... to her! Which was the
least expected
Was it love or something else?
Barely she could get it in her head.
She went with the flow...
Accepted him for all that had been and what he
was
Just for one thing…
It was the love she couldn't hide and halt.
And again, the wheel began to move
But this time it moved with pace
Cause this time... there were not two
But four hands which moved it in a race.

Heading towards a new start
Promising to never fall apart
'They' started afresh...
It was 'Their' love which was the thrust
And nothing could cut its flesh.
Together are they today
With so much love, compassion, and affection to
stay;
Hoping for time, future, and luck to be with
them
So that in the end, they can also say
"We lived happily ever after and in all ways."

Reverberating an Instant Crush

In the days of my youth, when girls filled my
school,
Amidst them stood a boy, caught my eye, oh so
cool.
Thought he was older, my crush, I kept it tucked
away,
But fate wove our paths closer, in a different
play.

Same age, same class, eyes met, no words
exchanged,
Just fleeting glances, hearts fluttered, feelings
estranged.
He had deep, dark eyes, and a smile with
dimples set,

In a blue shirt he looked his best, a style I can't
forget.

Years passed, new classes, we moved ahead,
Intelligent he was, I was the average instead.
One day, a party, we spoke, my heart took flight,
But he was into other girls, my hopes took a
slight plight.

Yet, moments shared, hints of something more,
But he chose another, my heart felt sore.
Still, I'd check for his car, before entering the
class,
Hoping he'd be there, despite what did pass.

Months turned, he disappeared, then reappeared,
Caught bunking, with his mom, truth now
cleared.
Eye contacts lingered, but I knew he was taken,
Quietly, I stepped back, my heart still shaken.

Time passed, school ended, paths diverged wide,
Lost touch, uncertain where life would ride.
Then one day, on my scooter, our eyes met fleet,
Memories flooded, emotions bittersweet.

Years flew, connected on social media's sway,
Secrets shared, music exchanged, a new day.

But he had a girlfriend, my feelings I tried to
tame,
Content with friendship, I doused the old flame.

Met a few times, talked now and then,
Late-night chats, his girlfriend's jealousy a yen.
He faced issues, they broke, his heart was frail,
He confessed he once liked me, nostalgia's tale.

Still, wrong timing played its part, paths divide,
He moved on, with someone, as did I, side by
side.
Friends now, distant yet close, in life's dance,
Teenage crush, a memory, a fleeting romance.

Different phases now, different lives unfold,
Some stories are not meant, yet remain gold.
That crush, that flutter, in youthful delight,
A chapter closed, yet it shines bright tonight.

A Diabolical Save

In a world ablaze, with no one to save,
You appeared like a whisper, my heart's only
crave.
Desire's strange dance, in foolishness we sway,
Never thought I'd meet you, in life's tangled
array.

But what a wicked game, we unknowingly play,
To feel this longing, night and day.
Such a wicked thing, to dream of your embrace,
Yet the world's harsh truth, leaves love no safe
place.

No, I don't wanna fall, where hearts break apart,
In this world that tears and pulls us apart.
For I'd never dreamed, I'd find someone like
you,
Yet I'd never dreamed, of losing you too.

No, I don't wanna fall in love's cruel game,
Where we risk it all, for a fleeting flame.
With you in my heart, yet the world tears us
apart,
In this cruel world's grasp, where nobody loves
no one.

So let's hold on tight, in this world so unkind,
Where love's a fragile thread, but it's all we can
find.
I never knew love, until you came into view,
Now I fear losing you, like the morning's first
dew.

No, I don't wanna fall, where hearts break apart,
In this world that tears and pulls us apart.
With you in my arms, though the world may not
see,
In this wicked game of love, just stay here with
me.

Friendship Sonnets

Natural Connections

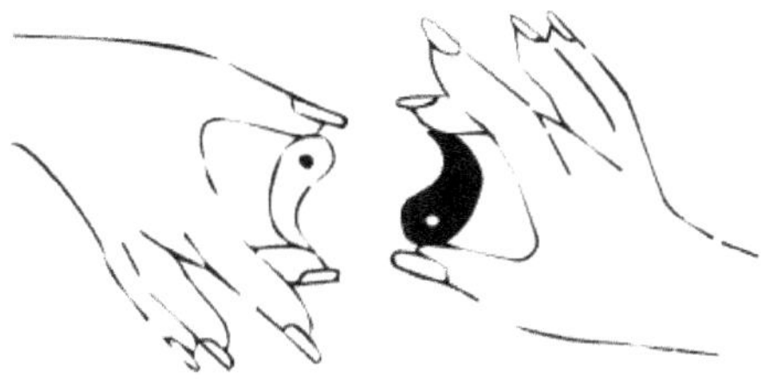

In a world of hustle and of haste,
There's a feeling that cannot be replaced.
When you meet someone and just click right through,
Talking freely, like you always knew.

Days pass by in endless chatter,
No effort needed, it's a natural matter.
Laughs come easy, conversations flow,
No judgments cast, just a soothing glow.

Peace and happiness fill the air,
As you build a bond beyond compare.
It's the joy of finding a true friend,
A connection that will never end.

So cherish those moments, pure and true,
When you find someone who clicks with you.
For in laughter and talks that are so fine,
Lies the beauty of a bond divine.

Friends Who Stay!

Life is like a party, a gathering so grand,
Inviting many souls to join, across the land.
Some arrive early, eager and bright,
While others come later, adding to the night.

Laughter echoes through the hours of joy,
Some join in merriment, a playful decoy.
Yet amidst the revelry, some may jest,
Not knowing the hearts they may test.

When the chaos settles, and quiet ensues,
A few remain, steadfast and true.
They help clean up, without a thought,
Of whose mess it was, or who had brought.

These friends are the gems, rare and fine,
Who stay through it all, rain or shine.
In the tapestry of life's intricate play,
It's those who stay to clean, who truly sway.

Blossoms & Thorns

In the rhythm of life's mysterious flow,
Time waltzes on, both fast and slow.
Amidst our bustling race's trace,
We seldom pause to embrace its grace.

Time, a silent, steady stream,
Brings together souls in a fleeting dream.
Yet, as swiftly as they meet, they part,
Like flowers crushed by a heavy heart.

Opposites collide, then bid farewell,
Leaving behind memories we once knew.
In our relentless march forward,
We often forget those we once adored.

Their absence is now a haunting regret,
Like roses plucked, we can't forget.
We journey on, uncertain and blind,
Unaware of what fate we'll find.

Some souls are roses, fragrant and bright,
While others are thorns, causing plight.
The pain of thorns, we wish to shun,
Yet their essence lingers when the roses are
gone.

In moments of strife, the scent prevails,
A reminder of love that never fails.
In joy and sorrow, it's our faithful guide,
Till time sweeps away the roses' pride.

As roses depart, thorns remain,
An unwelcome presence, causing pain.
Yet we cling to memories sweet and dear,
For in them, true friendship does appear.

So, let us cherish each fleeting hour,
Embrace the roses, and endure the thorns' power.
For in the garden of life, amidst its poses,
We find the beauty of friendship, akin to roses.

EPILOGUE

As the final page of "Ink & Constellations" turns, the journey through these verses draws to a close, but the echoes of the poems linger, like stars still shimmering in the night sky long after their light has reached us. Each poem, a constellation in its own right, has offered a glimpse into the myriad facets of our shared human experience, capturing the fleeting beauty of our struggles and triumphs.

In the quiet moments after reading, may you find yourself reflecting on the themes woven through these pages. Let the whispers of the verses guide you as you navigate your own path, reminding you that the intricacies of friendship, love, and ambition are not solitary pursuits but universal threads connecting us all, weaving a shared narrative that transcends individual experiences. The poems within this collection are more than just reflections; they are invitations to embrace the fullness of life with all its complexities.

As you step away from the world of "Ink & Constellations," carry with you the resilience and hope the verses have sought to impart. The beauty you've discovered in the chaos, the strength found in vulnerability, and the light in the darkness are not confined to the pages you've read—they are reflections of your inner universe.

May you continue to seek and find moments of profound insight in your everyday life. And remember, just as the constellations guide travellers through the night, so too do these poems offer direction and solace in the ever-unfolding journey of your own existence, a journey that is uniquely yours and deeply significant.
Thank you for embarking on this poetic odyssey. May the ink and constellations inspire you to shine brightly as you navigate the vast and wondrous expanse of your life's adventure.

Warm regards,
Ishita Arora